THE NATIONAL POETRY SERIES was established in 1978 to ensure the publication of five collections of poetry annually through five participating publishers. The series is funded annually by Amazon Literary Partnership, William Geoffrey Beattie, the Gettinger Family Foundation, Bruce Gibney, HarperCollins Publishers, the Stephen and Tabitha King Foundation, Padma Lakshmi, Lannan Foundation, Newman's Own Foundation, Anna and Olafur Olafsson, Penguin Random House, the Poetry Foundation, Amy Tan and Louis DeMattei, Amor Towles, Elise and Steven Trulaske, and the National Poetry Series Board of Directors.

The National Poetry Series Winners of the 2020 Open Competition

Dear Specimen
by W.J. Herbert of Kingston, NY
Chosen by Kwame Dawes for Beacon Press

[WHITE]
by Trevor Ketner of New York, NY
Chosen by Forrest Gander for University of Georgia Press

Borderline Fortune
by Teresa K. Miller of Portland, OR
Chosen by Carol Muske-Dukes for Penguin Books

Requeening
by Amanda Moore of San Francisco, CA
Chosen by Ocean Vuong for Ecco

Philomath
by Devon Walker-Figueroa of Brooklyn, NY
Chosen by Sally Keith for Milkweed Editions

Philomath

Poems

Devon Walker-Figueroa

MILKWEED EDITIONS

Published 2021 by Milkweed Editions
Printed in Canada
Cover design by Mary Austin Speaker
Cover art: "Cannon Beach, Oregon" by Erik Linton
22 23 24 25 26   6 5 4 3 2
First Edition

Milkweed Editions, an independent nonprofit publisher, gratefully acknowledges sustaining support from our Board of Directors; the Alan B. Slifka Foundation and its president, Riva Ariella Ritvo-Slifka; the Amazon Literary Partnership; the Ballard Spahr Foundation; *Copper Nickel*; the McKnight Foundation; the National Endowment for the Arts; the National Poetry Series; the Target Foundation; and other generous contributions from foundations, corporations, and individuals. Also, this activity is made possible by the voters of Minnesota through a Minnesota State Arts Board Operating Support grant, thanks to a legislative appropriation from the arts and cultural heritage fund. For a full listing of Milkweed Editions supporters, please visit milkweed.org.

Library of Congress Cataloging-in-Publication Data

Names: Walker-Figueroa, Devon, author.
Title: Philomath : poems / Devon Walker-Figueroa.
Description: First edition. | Minneapolis, Minnesota : Milkweed Editions, 2021. | Summary: "Philomath was
    selected for the 2020 National Poetry Series by Sally Keith"-- Provided by publisher.
Identifiers: LCCN 2020054958 (print) | LCCN 2020054959 (ebook) | ISBN 9781571315229 (paperback ; acid-free
    paper) | ISBN 9781571317629 (ebook)
Subjects: LCGFT: Poetry.
Classification: LCC PS3623.A359595 P48 2021 (print) | LCC PS3623.A359595 (ebook) | DDC 811/.6--dc23
LC record available at https://lccn.loc.gov/2020054958
LC ebook record available at https://lccn.loc.gov/2020054959

Milkweed Editions is committed to ecological stewardship. We strive to align our book production practices with this principle, and to reduce the impact of our operations in the environment. We are a member of the Green Press Initiative, a nonprofit coalition of publishers, manufacturers, and authors working to protect the world's endangered forests and conserve natural resources. *Philomath* was printed on acid-free 100% postconsumer-waste paper by Friesens Corporation.

for Jackie Walker

CONTENTS

I.

II.

III.

IV.

I.

Hell is a pure faith.
— C.D. Wright

Philomath

"Love of learning" is what
         Philomath means. This side of a ghost
town, what kids are here hang out
         in gravel parking lots & hunt
pixelated deer at The Woodsman. They break
         into gutted sanctuaries
of timber mills, looking for places to leave
         their neon aerosoled names. In Philomath,
Begg's Tires is the only place
         to buy new chains, Cherry Tree's the best
price on feed, & Ray's has everything
         from meds to milk to Lucky
Strikes & pocket knives. The only outlet
         in Philomath sells wood, the kind that grows
just here & in the holy lands. True
         Value boasts all the sturdy dead
bolts for when the back door's gone
         busted again. My friend
Megan is still giving out
         blow jobs to mechanics & drinking
red cough syrup until she doesn't
         care about her step-
dad walking around, covered in nothing
         but sweat & dirt. "Me & you are
gonna get trashed tonight," she says to me
         every night. I ask my dad if Megan can move

in & he says, "Twelve cats & two
        dogs are enough." In Philomath, I'd be lying
if I said people don't get saved
        every week at the Nazarene Church, where
Megan & I go to Vacation
        Bible School & sing about going "straight
to heaven or down the hole," where the pastor slips
        nylons over our faces & tells us to suck
pudding from a bucket just to show how far we'll go
        to be forgiven. We swallow it all
because this is how you get close
        to God in Philomath. When Megan's dad learns
she's saved & he's not, he teaches her
        a lesson about being
sorry & how God is not
        watching Philomath. On Monday, Megan's eyes
can hardly open & our school
        bans Liquid Paper & permanent
markers & the word
        "bomb," because they could cause us
to die before our time. Megan spends
        breaks in the bathroom & I know not
to follow her. I go to the library, where I check out
        A Season in Hell because they don't
have *Illuminations* & never will & I feel alone
        around all the smart kids who raise up
pigs to pay for college. They belong
        to 4-H & know how to sell living
meat to the highest bidder. They get made

fun of by people like Megan & me
& the boys who only wear camo & talk
about the beauty of a deer
spitting up its life & most anybody
the teachers have given up
on, which is nearly everyone. I care about
Philomath & its "Love
of Learning" bumper stickers that turn
invisible under mud, its historical
society that hangs
quilts over the walls of Paul's
Place (where loggers get Bottomless
Joe), that documents every haunting,
every sighting of a ghost, & Megan is still
in the bathroom stall, learning what it means
to be in Philomath for good.

Permission to Mar

Outside the house is the sound of becoming—
                                    the chirr of locusts, their low-
    lying electricity in the field, their inhuman
                                    hum accelerating into
        a revision of silence. Inside, I write
my name—the only one whose characters I know
                                    por corazón, and just by half, my *last*
        still incomprehensible—on the wall. All
            jagged and majuscular, all orange story-
        book shade of flame, inconstant color I
learn with light   pressure behind the crayon's tip
            recalls my mother's skin
        tone, with more force, belongs to the note
E (according to the method I am
        learning), consonant thrum of a slight
string I touch in her piano's   hull, highest
space of the treble's   F   A   C   E   I am wholly
        troubled as I scrawl, in this new   zone, perceiving
                                    I am *me* and all I take
    in exists merely   as this me, though without
    requiring me, every *you* also
                                    a *me*, and this is so, and this is so
        because I am allowed, for this not loud second, to be
my mother's call for me when I slip
                out of view—string of letters permitted to mar her
                    wall with my name

Golden

We are a kind
of sick that takes saving
up for, every day another
deposit in a bedeviled account
of history, the devil
being my father's blood
brother who's driven
our lot far from real
town & school &
the possibility of being
listed in a phone book
thick as Exodus. There
is talk of changing
our name to Golden,
as if we were a family plucked
from the pages of *What-
a-Jolly Street*, pastel place
where every daughter is
blonde, petti—
coated & crowned
in sausage curls, where
every son possesses
a blue bicycle & the name
Jimmy or Tommy—
anything ending
in "me." My sister

who goes by Joey says
the house is suffering
from a curse, the kind
that holds a soul
to soil, says
a figure nightly
flickers by our gate,
a woman who runs
at breakneck but doesn't move
anywhere. When we moved
the first time, it was
to a town known
widely for its wild
drug fest called Country
Fair. Once, at its local
diner, Our Daily Bread,
a wide-eyed woman
clothed only in blue
paint sat one pew
over, ordering stinging
nettle soup, & no one
batted a lash. But I would
take blue stoners any day
over ghosts that don't
know they're ghosts,
but keep reminding
you they're failing
to move toward light.
My mother has been known

to arm herself at night, tip-
toe in her nightgown down
the hall when the back
door slams & sourceless
footsteps begin falling
toward us. (After Toro,
our pit bull, got
a blood brother's bat to the head
out by the well, we promised
ourselves we were capable of killing
our kind.) But the footsteps are
just testament to the dead
never being the kind of gone
you think they are. In Old
Testament times, people killed
each other with stones
& hungry animals & pits
full of flames, with the building
of great marble
temples. People
were probably grateful
then, to leave this earthly
kingdom, not knowing
every life is an afterlife
& heaven is just a ghost
town that never ends. When
I finally learn to handle
my mother's re-
volver, I can only hit

the bullseye when I
pretend I'm Isaac
King, the man who shot
his face off in our barn.
In his day, when you
could pierce the dirt
with a flag & call
it yours, exiting this life
was a crime that could keep you
from sleeping anywhere
sacred. There are times
I whisper to our empty living
room, move toward
the light. Find a way
out of this valley named
for a family so dead
everyone calls them Kings.

Kings Valley

The neighbor is eating locusts again,
      as if a plague were just another
point of view, sitting out back of his caved
      two-story, squinting skyward, a cast
iron in hand, a mouthful of
      wings ground to dust. My sister's
busy too, straddling the fence, getting out
      our mom's gold pumps, spritzing her hair
into a hive of black. She's making the universal
      honk-your-horn sign at truckers who pass
with their loads of skinny firs bound
      to cross the Pacific. If they're lucky they get
a kiss blown over the yellow line, because
      they're only ever traveling
in one direction & that's away from Kings
      Valley, a place known for its dead
settlers & Xmas trees. There's a whole
      cemetery for land-claimers here, where
locals leave antlers & Hot Wheels & red
      polyester carnations on the graves
they like best. People with names like Nahum
      & Sarepta, who saw their kids give up
the ghost to ailments nobody can pronounce
      anymore, might be happy
to know they're still missed. The point
      of the steeple on the only church for miles

around blew down & no one's the means or the mind
        to fix it. My mother is trying to
be the good hostess
        she hopes I'll one day grow
into, schooling a girl named Mynda
        toward the GED we all say
stands for Goodness Ends
        in Degrees, showing her the difference
between the progressive & perfect
        tenses, how to interpret
the verse "touch me
        not, for I have not yet ascended," the necessity
of opening the day with a sorry for trespasses
        unwittingly made. I have a habit of trespassing
to see our neighbor's sow, the one who gave
        birth to thirteen piglets only
to crush them in her sleep. She's had so many litters
        over the years & they're all defecating
into the creek now, making us worry our wells
        will fail us. I also
have a habit of visiting his cat, the one he calls
        Confederate Gray, who licks the air
if you stroke her ribs. My sister asks me to cut
        her hair again & again we drop the locks
in the creek & hope it never stops
        moving away from us. It seems we'll get by
with our lie a little longer, if only
        because the nematodes are failing
to save the Yukon Golds & the thistle is

going to seed & Mark, a family
friend who happens to be hard
    up, is sleeping on the couch, asking us
to call him Lucky like it's Desert
    Storm all over again. He takes it
upon himself to *learn me*
    vigilance, which is to say, self
defense. He tells me to give
    him everything I've got,
but I've never done that
    for anyone, & I don't think I'm ready
to begin. His forearm finds its way
    to my throat & his knee goes right
between my legs. He holds me
    to the wall till I admit
I'm licked, which happens quick, but anyway
    humiliation's hardly real
when only John Wayne is watching
    from his lacquered saw blade on the wall
& anyway does anybody survive war
    without being won
over by the dream of decline? You can find us
    on ghosttowns.com, or you can find us
on A&E, re-running our stories
    about how haunted this place really is—
women waking up to translucent children
    braiding their hair, all those farmhands
who saw Old Man Cosgrove only visible
    from the waist up, who tells them

this valley is paradise & no one's
        told him otherwise. There's a store here
called *The* Store & it just quit
        selling gas because its holding
tanks are pure rust & won't take another
        drop. Still, you can purchase Dream-
sicles & Bud & home-
        cured jerky, & Charlotte who runs
the show will skin & quarter your kill for free
        if you bale her hay. She says
the locusts are in cahoots with their stinging cousins
        who inhabit the dirt & just recently flew
up my shorts & stung me till I stripped
        stark, till I climbed a live-
wired fence & ran two meadows only
        to find out I was amusing
the neighbor's pigs, who cooled in the mud,
        blinking away flies. My father got so pissed
he set the whole nest aflame, only
        the fire didn't stay
where he put it & so a season's worth
        of growth went up in smoke
& the locusts mourned & the scent
        of singed Rieslings lingered in my hair
for a whole week. He said it was lightning
        had struck, & Mynda wrote a song
in honor of the crop. I remember
        only the phrase "portentous
clouds vandalizing blue." (The insects remained

unscathed.) I admit I'm proud
of my sister for mastering false
        lashes & liquid liner, for painting cat eyes
that'd make Audrey jealous
        if she were alive & smoking
as if it weren't deadly & dancing
        with Fred Astaire. There isn't much to check out
at The Store, but *Funny Face* is one
        option & my sister & I know every
line by heart, every step
        & throb of Technicolor. So we watch it again
while Dad feeds the burn barrel yesterday's
        news & the high-gloss catalogues
he doesn't want us
        to be tempted by & the boxes of cereal
that always say, "Better Luck
        Next Time" & sometimes it seems
the future has a habit of repeating itself.

Out of Body

Have you ever watched a person burn

                        what's left of the person they love   I have

       stood by   I have caught the flames and pulled them up

into my skull   my father poured the fuel   over

the heap of my mother's possessions   ladder-back rocking chair   where

          she sat on sleepless nights and nursed   unspoken injuries

her hundred   blouses color of bone   rickety hand-me-down chest   claw-

footed and full   of sepia scowls and strips   of the old comic

"Love Is ..."   her silk scarf fluttering like an oriflamme   her

         lock of hair   color of mine   bound in a blue ribbon tangling

with itself   everything ablaze   under the quick

        touch of match   my father does not look back

at the light he has made   my role to keep an eye

on what is left   to burn into oneness   the searing particulate   I

       think of the fuel   how it exists

to push the heat back   into my mother's chair   how the light climbs

         each rung

the flame seeming   to want   up and out of its own

need to consume   what frames the light of its own unmaking

      breathe in the ash   chest

chair

        faces   no   bigger than

fingerprints   flame-licked   arms   feet

                auburn   curls

     what   the air cannot hold

        it leaves on the tongue

After Birth

Reed, who's got one strike   left before he gets
life, tells me afterbirth   is what the cougars are after.
  "Lambing season," he says,   "plus, placenta's a delicacy
to a cat." I try to explain how   intent they were,

how their intentions appeared
                 to involve me, but Reed won't hear
a word. My mother takes me   at my word & won't
    let me leave the house. So I learn
to regret my story, sit indoors
    for weeks, watching   for hunters, only to find

    what's hunted: the gray   diggers interring green
walnuts at the feet of the tree   they fall from. Now
     all I can think of is blood,   how we first feed
on it without knowing   we feed on it

or that it possesses   a plan all its own. Every girl
       I know has started, nicknamed it
  Florence or Flo or *The Red Badge*
of Courage. It'll be years   for me. When a doctor
   finally says, "You've fallen so far
        off the growth chart, I'm worried

    you won't find your way back,"
I'm fourteen & can still go out

shirtless without causing   a stir. "Eat more
butter," he says, but I don't
          yet believe what I eat will help me hate
my body any less. Reed doesn't hate
          his kids. He loves them

     too much is the story. People tell me
to avoid him, but I don't.   His flocks graze the fields I drag
my shadow over & I   have nothing better
          to do than gaze at interminable
feeding, mumbling Exodus
               under my breath, some passage

     about bearing false   witness. & I think I know
by now that *knowing* involves   the senses turning a touch
     licentious. My parents   haven't known each other
in years & no one wants   to know me either. A tree falls

in the woods. Con-   sensus leaves us cold, etc. *Green
     Eggs and Ham,* I really dislike   that kid's book, with all
its I-would-nots & could-nots   on boats & in woods,
     all its reds & its greens inter-   mingled, muck of inks

you should never swallow.   A doctor hands me
          a copy, says, "go   enjoy" & pulls a plastic curtain
between us. I'm three & can't yet read   any word on my own
     but "God." He reaches   his hand, gloved

                    green, inside my mother & says,
          "What about this weather we are
.having?" Just between
                              us, I warn the story's star not to touch
its plate, but in the end   it'll do what the good Dr. has
          scripted. I throw the book. My mother stops

   singing beneath a stream of steaming
                              water, a red-black mass dehiscing
     at her feet. "Find
                    your father," she commands, so I run
through yellow meadows, yelling   his name, his name,
   which the hills give back   to me, though he can't

hear them from the other side   of this state. On the other
   side of this state, my mother   finds her first horse.
It is 1980, decade   of the single-wide & no-
   children-in-the-   picture. Just a mare called Chianti

who dies one year   before I'm born. Her heart,
          size of a child's   globe, fails while foaling,
something involving a decayed   length of intestine & great
     pain. My parents take   great pains to save

                    her, but the foal will lose
his mother   the instant   the air   enters his chest.
   In Egyptian hieroglyphs, "I" can be rendered
     as a single   reed & "meadow" as a row of three
reeds bound by a flatline   of horizon. I know little,

even now, though enough   to say my name & know it's not

    mine, but just   some inadvertent testament

          to my mother's love   of horses & good

breeding. In an ancient *Seventeen*

               Magazine, an English girl of means

straddles a dappled pure-   bred bearing my name.

   Seventeen, the age I am   when my interior starts giving up

the way it's meant to,   with blood, & thanks

   only to pregnant mares held   captive, their urine stolen

   for the green tablets I'm made

                    to swallow. & though I feel

like a martyr outgrowing   martyrdom when it happens,

   a sacrifice of sorts still takes   place inside me. I

am the first to admit I'm kind   of a poser sometimes, like when

            I convince my friend Ann I've started,

      when in fact, I've only lifted

   my mother's lipstick to tint   my underpants the right

shade of red. Sure, I've begun   to forget my mother's

   writing as it appears   in *Arabian Horse World*, some piece

     on giving   birth & up & tricking a strange

mare into caring for a foal

         not hers by painting it up, by daubing

it down, in the afterbirth of her still-

            born. What more could one ask for?

My mother once rubbed moonshine on my gums to numb the pain
        appearing inside me. Moonshine, the name   given the foal
                dressed in after-   birth & therefore breathing.

The Blood's Unwritable Psalm

My body is just the story it tells
in order to be true. The moon goes on

enlarging the ballad of its fall, pretending
                    it's innocent as a cloak

draped over a virgin's shoulders. I was once
virginal before I was tangible, and my voice

swaddled me in what I've learned to call
refrain. If I'd been born in the shape of

a boy, I might have been
                    named after trees so old

they are only the sounds   we make for them.

II.

Hymns are not allowed here.
The air will not hold them.
—ARTHUR RIMBAUD

My Materia

Each day she opened.
                    with a blessing   so inherited it was more
cadence than melody,
more supplication than belief   she held   my hand, my sister's, we a chain
   our murmurations long—   *a kingdom a kingdom a kingdom*   become
echolalic   sin and syntax refracted   as the folded hands in her
favorite oil painting   (hands seeming to emerge   exit   their frame and in
so doing shatter, merge   with distance and the light that makes it
              known)
I once fixed the image of her brain
        (magnetic/resonant)
          to my father's light
table, the one he used in crafting maps, to find   the small stain inhabiting
the corner of her/the   mind in which place-finding occurs   in which place
     cells ignite in the image of the navigable, of the   at-hand
her eyes were white and large and seemed   impatient as planets waiting to be
   released into the preordained   ellipses of orbit,
and the cortex—
     its deep folds holding her ability   to abide in formation,
revise   the elongating now
into the now-and-again
I touched the spot   no bigger than a blot of ink   this
place in us that cannot know it is   being touched   I cried
             without restraint
              at the local aquarium when
          she informed me

                                        the jellyfish I was
                                                attempting to sketch
                                        lacked awareness
of its motions, of the lambent bloom
beneath its clear billowing skin, its skein of tentacles unfurling
                                                toward particles it could lift
                        to the mouth, the mouth
                                high up within the selfless bell of the body,
the way it contracted
and expanded its bulb, each narrowing an acceleration, each opening
                                                a slowing down,
an invitation to be nourished
                by matter unknown and unremembered
each fish became to me   time-lapsed, a petal moving surfaceward
    whose elegance was useless as my need   to preserve it
beauty merely   existence carrying on and carrying on
(the way the blood's fervor can outlast the mind's)
                                        she uncrossed her legs, un-
                                            laced her fingers
                                    from her fingers in order to place
                                        a warm palm on my head, at-
                                    tempt to dulcify   still
                                    I made a terrible   scene
so that an information   assistant crossed the room, asked if everything was
        alright   yes   yes   years
later, I found my-
        self in the same   city as *Materia*, painting wherein all planes exist
        pellucid, irradiated

by a warmth that cannot be said   to be   external, in which the human and the in-
        human (but alive)
               writhe in place, oscillate
below and within
                  the artist's mother, who is the subject, her every line bending
as though pure   luster cambering up   into an open, unseeing
                            eye that, too, once found
its way   into a scene   fragmented and aswarm   the day
was warm   when I set off to see it, she
called me long   distance, over-   seas, to in-   form me a girl from *home*
was found   buried   alive in an oil drum
                   cruelty always at hand   my
        mother said, sooth-   said
          I would draw harm
          and she would live
             through it
      still I summon the buried
          girl in my less
               conscious hours
her nails dark-dappled   crimson, cobalt, malachite, chipped
        from clawing at the interior
of the drum, and I am there   inside the steel vessel   beside her I have no need
to breathe, no hands   with which to lend   service, nor voice
and all the body wants is not   to be held   fast in this earth, but to give
        breath permission   to find its source   again
struggle is the only sound
slowing till it takes the tempo of a hymn
my mother once sung in a secret   society (Job's   Daughters) in which

                          young girls gather
robed in white, assemble
                    their still narrow frames in the shape of a cross, and my mother
                                        at the point of inter-
                    section, the place where one line of virgins touches another in order
        that the shape might not warp over-   much, that its humming
arms remain   immalleable and outstretched, proving
                    perfection, though the girls are in-   capable of keeping
                                        the light out of their eyes—they bend
one way, another, their   loose robes shimmering as they shuffle to
                                        and to and fro, their frayed
        attempt at symmetry, in order that the sacred take   shape, in order
                    that the taken   *daughters, wife, health, merciful*
                maker could live   in the sacrament of the mind
        a little longer (the hymn that is being
                    forgotten begins *Be Thou*

Of Gut & Gold

My harp is weary heavy
& I can hardly move
it on my own, even now
I'm grown & gone
far from what my father calls
his Canaan. He strums
what strings he can from time
to time, sounds out "Joy
of Man's Desiring" despite
the fact six strings have
snapped & middle C has
fallen to B. It happened before
I knew it, this learning
to play an hour's worth
of minuets, what made him
say, "You're the show
horse & I'm just the work one."
He traded a stand of trees
for what he knew I'd teach
myself. It's easy to replay
the scene in which I play
the harp he says I'll own
someday, my sister's bow see-
sawing over her violin,
our mother on the upright,
& him so near the fire

he'd built, his fingers
laced, eyes closed tight, torso
rocking like the wand
of a metronome. Maybe
what I wanted was to teach
him a note could still
be new, be worth
a forest trucked to Boise—
but I've never won
that argument with God
& it took ten years to know
just what he'd done. None
but my harp teacher
could tell you now the tale
wherein a girl is given
a harp with forty strings of gut
& one of gold. Her father in
the story's always dying
of some mythic sickness
you can only deem a curse, hands
wilting on dwindled wrists, teeth
crumbling from gums
like bits of gypsum. Each time
she made that gold string sing,
her father's youth would move
a little closer. Even the wrecked
tunnel of his throat revived
its ballads & his hands
unfurled like lilies dropped

in tea. In the end, she traded one
wellness for another,
grew ancient as her father
grew new. I imagined he lacked
a music of his own, thought
he couldn't read
the language Mozart spoke,
as if that daughter could have
said a thing to heaven & been heard
just because she'd taken up
her psalmodies so young. I didn't
yet know he had a secret
music, my father, strange
tongue planted
where I couldn't go. I heard him speak it
first to the man who helped him
cut down trees. Ayúdeme,
he called, as if I'd never learn
the song of something falling into use.

We Said Our Common Ancestor Was Eve

(a canzone for Nan)

Chance made Nan   my friend & the end
of my love for Gregorian chants. I thought   to pose
as an answer to her   question about heaven's distended
intention to make a singed   fruit &, therefore, self. Wend
us a new way, we'd meant to say   to the sky, but went
our ways before the prayer romanced us. Fanciful blend
we were, our puerile   hands fondling what lends
virginity its antidote. We doted as noxious toxins
dote on the dead, fed   our dreams inevitable sins,
the kind you lie about till you grow   mean, start bending
your will to an order   you'd reinvent this instant
if only it were yours. (It is   yours, as this taunt's

half mine.) Nan will not forgive   me the distance
I don't remedy. Her older brother got her   suspended
from my life, blew up a Home   Ec room—instance
of premature fascination. His face   an ancient trance
fastened to teenage bone. Now   he has a smile. I suppose
fatherhood alters   a boy. It was Nan's job to entrance
the steer in her father's field, slip   inside & dance
the hay down to its trough. Often   enough, we'd frequent
that field, straddle its fence, let the bovines quench
their thirst for salt   on our naked feet. We'd watch ants

colonize dirt below our half- anointed ankles. Frantic
the heifers became the day the steer was harvested. Entrance

of bullet into left temple left us holding what, instants
before, composed the animal's thoughts, scintillas
of synapses blown dim, ants so quick to eat the lurid bits
bone-blank. We marveled at the warm slick tinting
our palms incarnadine as what transcends
lowliness, is slit
open ceaselessly. After the slaughter, we played the sluts
our parents warned us against becoming, Nan's adipose
breast buds bluing in the bath, my mouth imposing
rouged parentheses on her shoulder. This a slanted
version of another game wherein we'd go delinquent,
stalk her deaf mother Marnie for hours. Rules went

if she saw you, you stopped dead, underwent
alchemy (your body a plank cluttering the present tense
& the eye of a maddened maker). Infrequently,
Marnie would speak to me, tell of the convent
in which she learned to read lips, synecdochic
syllables extrapolated into sense, kind you breed into covenant.
Nan & I took to descending into the daylight basement
wherein her brother lived— a boy abased, amended
into a man & soon to be reprimanded for this life. We'd end
up snooping—unfolding his underpants, planting deliquescent
leftovers in his sheets, fingering a bundle of tubes poised
on his roll-top. (I've always been pre-disposed

to loving   a well-assembled object.) He'd get back, dose
me with an apathy that rivaled   scorn, but for Nan invented
a riskier reply, put her inside   the oven—closed
& locked it. That morning,   Marnie was supposed
to bake bread, but forgot   to hit heat, entranced
as she was by a girl on TV   who, indisposed
by bad blood, married young. (It was   symbolic.) She dozed
through the bride's translation   into static light, her lapsed
life a thing leavening   toward its own collapse.
"I sweated & swore. I filled   the kitchen full of woozy
cries," Nan told me. But "children will play" is how we end
the story. She spends   these days dissecting cadavers, mending

what a body can't. How could she   forgive this distance? (Amen.)
I didn't end up playing "All Creatures Great   & Small" at her wedding,
on my harp, though I said I'd do   it, though I shook
off her expired vow to revise   our lives into a loneliness rent
only by sharing it. I think she must continue   to smell of currants
drying on their stem in some field   where *to singe* is still *to sing*.

Out of Body

I envy the air

It neither marks nor mourns
        its own passage but dashes blind

through newborn throats and never
        notes the terrible

pitches to which it gives way but just keeps
moving keeps conforming

to each curvature with all
        the acquiescence of a sigh let loose in sleep

      sky   *zephyr*   *xylem*   *why*

It carries the weight of every cry   every gesture
never heeding how   long each one

(say *I*   say hew   say panacea)

takes to ring   takes to die

~

There are times I think I can hold

it inside   me forever
          this air   other
times only a second
                    when my life is still

new and my memories   absent as untouched
skin I hold until it goes

stale and useless inside me   I

have feared it too (as now forgotten
          kings feared

the maker they could not make themselves
sense)   its invisibility and necessity balance

in algebraic perfection filling   the mouths of the
                    living as it swells
the bellies of the dead   rouses the neurons

and tympana   and those tiny molluskan chambers that
          coiled so quietly behind
the eyes   wait to make each sound
     drop of a hand

hum of a wire

whir of a reel

carry

My Father's House

After hitchhiking many miles to my father's house, I asked for a glass of water. He told me it was safe here. I have killed all the pests, all of the rats and the flickers and those iridescent beetles that used to move through the sky like a glittering rain cloud, he said. He handed me a glass of his perfect well water and informed me I would never find the like in the city. I nodded. The water was warm and smelled like soil. It tasted like nothing at all. I asked my father how he was making do, and when he pretended not to hear me, I asked him if he had a cube of ice. Help yourself, he said. Feeling grown up, I opened the freezer and reached inside. But there was no ice. Only an ancient piece of wedding cake and my first pet cat sealed in a plastic bag. I opened the bag and ran my fingers through the rigid hair. Each notch in the spine felt like an angry knuckle. I could stay awhile, if you'd like, I said. But he was looking out the window at his freshly mowed fields, taking account of his labors.

Gray Diggers

The first letter I ever wrote
        was addressed to GOD WITH US & I
put my location down as being
        Philomath because it's the closest
you get to civilization out here, as in you
        can get your weekly fill
of diesel there, fix your dog, stock up
        on bullets & Maker's & live
bait. I dropped the finished
        missive into Onion Creek which runs
behind our house, a house
        that belonged to horses
before it belonged to a devil-
        worshipping woman who plowed
her Ford into the kitchen
        window, or so my father says
if talk is slow & you ask him why
        the floors don't touch
the walls the way they should. We put up
        with all our gap invites
in from the rain, which is mostly gray
        diggers—breed of squirrel that squeezes
into your walls & dies
        there in protest to your appetite
for its kind. Rick, our hand,
        as he calls himself, has started pissing

in the orchard on the pioneer
　　　plum because he can't breathe
right in the house, with the cats & the rabbit
　　　& its unlucky cousin still
stuck in the wall, & this
　　　from a man who smokes a Marlboro Red
every hour of his life. I'm grateful for
　　　the company, the mindless knock-
knock jokes, the scent of his leather jacket
　　　in the closet. He has a way of being
the loneliest person you've ever met, besides
　　　yourself, except when he's holding
his Maverick & teaching you how
　　　to aim for the hay man's heart,
the one who wears the blue
　　　button-up he forgot you
bought him for his birthday. One day,
　　　he'll give me his hand-
gun, or so he promises, but I'm not
　　　in a hurry. (My father leaves
the revolver he likes
　　　least under my bed, behind what's left
of Monopoly & Sorry & a jigsaw
　　　of bungalows whose bay windows glow
like the suitcase in *Kiss Me*
　　　Deadly.) The first letter I ever wrote
I wrote because I was told to pray
　　　without opening my trap. I did it
in cursive, because every letter is more

beautiful when touching
the others that make it mean. "I'm sorry,"
        I said, to a fraction of God & the dust-
less husk of a moth I'd held
        too long. I've never held a digger in
my hands, though they make themselves
        at home & known, & Rick
has promised to open up
        the walls if it comes down
to it. He says he's tempted to open
        fire on the bathroom wall
just to get the message
        across. He wants to reach
inside the failing plaster, pull the ring-
        leader into the light, make her
forget why she's raising Cain & a family
        in a house that isn't hers.

Out of Body

Perdition collects   in the corner of this family
        room where delicate images go to last
    where light cannot
reach   how many times must I
        slip the photograph from its frame
press my fingers to its edges and pretend they are not
            sharp   the face
of my mother   smiling in accordance with tradition
the counterfeit   knowledge I still
                keep with me like memories of being
loved   all that half-digested guesswork   send me
to the corner one more time   force my nose
into the shadows   I find   so repulsive the need
to conflate image with existence   history
with belief   my father tells me she hated being
touched   *a wonder you were ever born*   he cannot believe
the ground contains her   shiver of envy
in his throat the dirt   body of particulate cruelty
as though it could feel what it held   as though it could tell
what filled its hollow places my   father speaks a scene that lies
buried   her father   lineman, herder, jack-
of-all-trades   his weathered hands tightening
around her fourteen-year-old throat   *I love you*
        you little bitch   the words
congregated hovering   over
                her lips   as if they belonged

there   she burned
a photograph of her father   once   his cowboy face
              etched with sunlight
his hairline mouth closed   tight around a smoldering
end   the way his body curled   into itself
                          the shade of green it turned
before crumbling into ash   the smile
on her face   crescent of rage when he died
              he left her   all he had a little plot
of land with bad soils   a stick-built that smelled like a lifetime
of cheap smokes   chest full of molding daguerreotypes
(how well it held the Wild West with its landmark agony
of blood-stained trails   its multitude of blurred
cattle   knit of horns   army of men   ropes dangling
        from belts   from teeth   from bovine throats
in loops   )   all that I did not say   remains   in my mouth

III.

What are you there? Your names?
—GLOUCESTER, *KING LEAR,*
ACT 3 SCENE 4

Ascent

Down by the creek
    named for its sweat-
scented roots, my sister teaches me
    to relieve the ache I imagine
God gives only the wicked. Here
    is where to place
your touch, your breath, your troubling
    assent. Delight
relived—the anticipated end
    of our exploit—comes with gloaming,
the appearance of lives
    you don't see lived in
full sun. The swallow
    you cannot name. (What I'm learning
to call pleasure is more
    akin to belief.) My sister slouches
over when the soughing
    ceases, says, "No one has to know
this place exists."

Drain

At seven, I learned the logic of cedars—
their relentless failure
to live, the frail
flame they leave for you
to cut down & to curse.
The locals called the new
condition rust. "It'll open up
our view of Marys Peak,"
they said. My father blamed his blood
brother, brother
who'd bought up all
the land around our land,
who, as a boy, delighted
in harvesting
wings from flies. Funny
to think of a thing named
for what it cannot do. I've never spoken
to the man, though I know
he's mastered
eleven tongues & runs a language
school near Okinawa. "Once,
he bragged about hiding
cameras in the showers
of that school," my father
says in trying
moments, as I try to appear lost

in thought. I suspect
the blood brother can carry
a captivating conversation
in the language I am
trying to learn, language
of a branch that lets you
express the thought "I hear
heat" or "I taste
heat," which makes "to feel"
end up feeling a touch
inadequate. "Blood is
thicker than water"
is a saying my mother
despised when she was
running our house like an inn
for the insane. She loved nearly
any animal that wasn't
cut out for living—like
orphaned fawns & withdrawn
addicts she'd find
trembling at rest
stops along Route 20, like cedar
waxwings that mistook glass
for the space that lives
behind glass. Under the last
incense-cedar in the back
yard, we had a whole
boneyard of birds—
Toby, Thelma, Obadiah. We didn't know

their sex. We didn't know
why they camped all winter
long when they had bodies
that could carry them
some place warm & somehow full
of promise. *Mti* means
tree & *mtu* is *person*
in the tongue I try to hold
as if it were mine. In the tongue
I was born to, I was to be called
Forest, but then I wasn't born
a boy & you can guess
the rest of the story. Everyone wanted
a brother for my sister.
I wanted a brother for all
of time, but my parents'
tepid tries ended
in prematurity & my mother
believed these losses due
to the blood brother standing
beside the driveway, cursing
her, screaming
whore every time she'd open
the gate. At the time,
I didn't really know
what *whore* meant, nor
that it used to be a homophone
to *hour*, a fact not lost
on Elizabethans. Also not lost

on Elizabethans was the value of public
dissection, a theater
of which my father would be
fond. I say fond, given his love
of forensic science
shows, in which crimes get duly
accounted for while we feast
our eyes. "Do you see that?"
he once asked over dinner, pointing
his fork at the screen
over which flashed the image
of a lone limb (feminine,
etiolating on a Floridian
beach), "The hair keeps growing
after death!" My middle name is
Elizabeth, which means "My God
is an Oath." So is my mother's.
Was. So was her mother's
mother's & such is my book
of #s, so full of aimless begats.
According to Psalm 92,
the righteous shall flourish
like a cedar of Lebanon. I always
assumed the word
shall meant in my lifetime, that is,
when my life was a rehearsal
for eternity. The infected
fronds of a cedar smell
sweet when July touches

them, so sweet you swear
they can't be dying now
or ever, though you know
their fall is ripening
underfoot. The root
—*ake* means both *his & hers*
in the language
I am trying to learn, meaning
perhaps an object is altered
little by the hand that holds
it, by the many aching parts
attached to the hand & to
its holding. The blood brother had
at some point promised
to have & to hold & had
two daughters whose names escape
me, but end in
—*ko*, with whom I'm not
friends & might
never be, though I hear
they make art & suspect
they are kind. In Drain,
Oregon, in the last summer
of the cedars' lives, I found a kind
of kinship at Son Shine
Camp & climbed high up
on a cross in the middle of a dying
forest. You could smell
the orange needles as they fell

lightly at your feet as false
eyelashes. You could feel
sunshine seeping
through trees that couldn't feed
on light or water
anymore. In the game, my # was
called, meaning I was to be
crucified & a boy
I wouldn't exactly call
my neighbor squeezed
a ketchup bottle
in both hands & whispered, "Don't
forget to shout *forgive them,*
Father, 'cause they don't know
what they're doing & don't
worry, Dee. It'll be so quick & just
like getting your blood
drawn." I said, "I won't forget."

Damp Room

I.

It's entirely up to me to remember

                 what you said. But all I recall is water,
flour, strained   yolk adding

up to something beaten and inedible. I place
        my ear to your stomach,   where
excess warmth gathers in the name

                 of the body's clandestine
ritual of diminishment. I'd crouch
      at your feet in the shower, allowing   what pale

lather ran in runnels from your hair, elbows, breasts, wrists down

over   me because the parameterized world
        let slip   its hold over
us   in the face of mantled contentment. I meant

to tell someone   in time, the last   time we were
       alone, but the room seemed aware
               it held us, as in, it held

fast the me that rubbed your hands until a useless
blush idled in your palms, and I

looked past slack lips long
   enough to know they belonged to   nothing I can mend.

II.

                        Did you know a whole city
could be a damp room? All its illuminated   manuscripts,
vivisected, hanging
            on lines, as if they were slips
                        rinsed and held up to the wind
of a person walking by, a de-

humidifier humming on low for all the dismantled
                lapis, a lip   brush collecting particulate after-
                    math from a gilded B. The year was

no longer young: the Arno rose in accordance with orographic
                    law, lapping at the city's Gates of

Paradise, pulling loose the creation   scene from its rightful
            cell, scene in which a bronze father lifts his conscious

daughter from the breast of his unconscious
                        son. It is a kind of birth, an impossibility

annulled by belief and brushstrokes and undisclosed
  fingerprints, by unmerciful years and the volatilizing away of

mercury until a nameless   apprentice goes   mad in the making

      of gates, until

                only gold remains visible, and you
must lean so close—as if you were
                              preparing your eyes for a curtain

                call, or attempting to peer into the flaw
each line and pore and follicle is—

Persistence of Vision

I, too, was the prison
       guard—bribed by faith
into bringing a new-
       born to the cell of a martyr
hell-bent on gratifying
       the silence she deemed
divine. I am
       the one who watched her eat
what we call the *free*
       banquet, but only after
the infant's mouth gave up
       the warmth of his mother's
milk. I don't remember
       the name she gave
the child, but it appeared
       to have the hunger of a man
who spends his hours building
       walls that will one day be believed
holy or justified or merely
       useless-beautiful. Perpetua held
the bald head up, as if it were cast
       of bronze, so cumbersome
it seemed, so beyond human
       need. Still, her
death meant more

to her than any life, for life
is not so permanent
    as its reply. "Do you see
the vessel?" she asked
    her father, the father
who stooped and wrung
    his hands in the damp cell's
air. "Can it be called
    other than it is?" The day
arrived, resigned to its reoccurrence;
    and the executioner
watched his aim forsake
    him till Perpetua raised
the blade to her throat, said, "Cut here."

/

To ensure the convergence of images, place
    the thaumatrope stem between the palms.
Proceed to rub the palms
    together as furiously as possible, as if you are stranded

in the woods without matches, as if many lives
    depend upon this friction, and you will / witness
the naked oak find its lithographic
    leaves, the empty / vase its levitated arrangement

of freesias; even the swallow will concede
    to its cage, knowing enclosure is only

an extension of warmth, the exact

                     magnitude of which your ear encounters when you touch it

against the belly of a form recently filled

                           with the kind of movement you can see. Leave
your face there / long enough—the fugitive

                        warmth you feel will be your own.

/

I drive to the lookout you never   tired of. Cape Perpetua. The sky
          is rare, as in, unburdened of rain, and I
                 buckle up the bag of you, as if a bad
driver could still   disassemble you. I let myself
imagine the color blood turns as it boils down past   liquidity, down
to what cannot be said
to be needed any-   more; though I do imagine   the mauve dress I slid into
          one foreign morning, all its bronze bugle beads
sewn by hand, its pleats of taffeta pressed past
               perfect. It was more than I could pay, but I paid—

/

When I sleep, I'm many
things, sometimes a lamp shedding
her halo on the scene
of a crime no one knows
to call a crime. Other
times, I'm the wall-

paper stamped with wilting
irises bound in brown
ribbons. Other times, I'm
the ether reaching inside
a child whose speechlessness
remains unclaimed, looking
to find what's left of wonder.
But lately, I'm a dormitory
full of nightgowned girls, and I
burn so fast no one can touch
me, not by my searing
knobs nor my blistering
parquet. My walls oxidize
so rapidly, the furniture doesn't know
why, and the girls
pound their fists on my locked
windows, raising what voices are left
them. They want to know why
the streets outside me still exist.

/

    I spread it   over your bed, like a brushstroke meant to stay
there, and it stayed   there till you hid it safely   away, awaiting
    the right occasion. But the occasion was never   right, and when it arrived
it was only a flash of light no eye could see, a searing

                convergence of nylon and the U-
    shaped hyoid, two silver   fillings, the floating
        ribs, unharvested—   If

I had to give   a swatch, say, to match   that dress to its day, I'd gather
a handful of dead man's bells—knowing as I do how they run
            rampant up this crazy   drive toward the parapet, the parapet

/

*In my absence, everyone / describes me / as saintly, and I / can only think
of* The Song / *of Bernadette, in which there is a body / of water that drinks
up sickness as a plant drinks up the light / we orbit and fear, making of it nourishment.*

*My shadow continues to accompany / me, as if it were my friend and not / ready
to thin, dim, double, and depart in the hours I need most to be / reminded
I remain. In my absence, my blood / knows its place, and my name / is nothing like lament.*

/

I thought the scent of singed Rieslings would never leave
me, my pores, nor would the deep-dwelling hymenoptera
cease their exodus—each population crackling, aswarm, helixing up and out of
the soil—miraged membrane of impending
ash, the August sky gave up
its azure as what lay beneath gave up its green. My mother's
fists flew high and at their highest lifting burst
open, released a brief bronze haze of lately-turned
earth—so quickly swallowed by the rage of orange and onyx
underfoot. Her voice, too,
flew high, though indecipherable within
a polyphony of hums and spattings and snapping
strings of a pure heat's speed. I ran the length of three

parched meadows, bare feet pricked purple by thistle whose pith
my heels ground down to pounce, before
I reached the landline, before I
filled the perforated mouthpiece with what
my face couldn't keep
to itself, and a girl's distress call kept skipping, *it's spreading, it's spreading*
too quick for us. We're alone—

/

      where I'll unfasten you from this seat   you don't need any-
more than you need my telling   you you'll feel
      between sand and stone-ground wheat   in my hands, that the secret

       of this bloom lies   in its ability to send
the blood's metronome into that trance that's sometimes needed
      just to keep the body   in time with its scheduled extinction.

Curse of Bodie

> "Please find enclosed one weatherbeaten old shoe.
> The shoe was removed from Bodie during the month of August 1978 . . .
> My trail of misfortune is so long and depressing it can't be listed here."
> —*anonymous "curse letter" sent to the Bodie State Historic Park*

Bodie is the first ghost town   I've met that makes people want
to visit it. They'll pay to cross   an ocean just to press
their faces to its fissured windows & take in
century-soiled sheets   no body will rise from
again. The beds in Bodie continue to be made
priceless by disuse as I   wander its streets with a childhood
friend. She poses now   before brothels & chapels
evacuated of howls & hymns & sins of every sort   while I snap
up the faces she makes   (as if for me). The wind is
up. The sun too. I wind the film   for another exposure as I rise
on tiptoe to glimpse   a bottle kept from emptiness
by a sip's worth of whiskey.   She whispers, "I bet you
anything some employee steals   inside the house at night
to fill it up" & I nod, feeling   she's right, whether "it" is
the bottle or   the house. Sure,   time is telling
its finest lies   in Bodie, where saloon girls still croon
from the other side   & the shiver of dry grass
makes you think   of a record dark & grooved
slipping from its sleeve. So   our steps drive rusty nails
a touch deeper   into the dirt as we pass
a leaning shed. So the mortuary still stands   up & for a form

of closure the rest of Bodie   won't obey. The scent
those bodies must've made   in the summer,
in the summer . . .   We look through another
window to find yet another   window carved in the lid
of some little kid's coffin & start   to doubt
if dying can even cure one   of her fears. In the museum
shop, we bend over letters that bemoan   failed kidneys & jobs
& vows, each scrawled trial accompanied   by a fragment of Bodie
bent on getting back   at its holder just to get back
to Bodie, where death's the only duty   you're expected
to perform. "Arrested   decay" is the state Bodie claims
to live in, if any place can be said   to live, to claim. I eye
the oxidizing can lids littering   the ground, begging to be
held, but trust the curse   letters to be true because I get
no coin is worth   a fishhook embedded in the eye,
nor an unearthed nail the only life   I'll ever get.
But how's it possible   to be in Bodie & not
spirit away some bit of it as you go?   Or maybe being
here is how   the curse begins. I lower myself
to the ground   to examine a mouse recently cured
of Bodie, drying in the sun, its hide   an outgrown coat
its bones just won't quit   wearing. "If we're still virgins
in two years," my friend   once mused, as we sprawled
on her double bed, lamenting   the vastness of our innocence,
"we could lose it   to each other." Like a child,
I prod what rots   & can't help it. Ants crawl
from the mouse & I start   to linger over the particles of Bodie
clinging to the soles & tongues   of our boots, thinking this thin film
might delete us from the world   of sunlight & luck. "I don't like

that my name is a place I haven't been   to," I state
to my friend, after reading   about William S. Bodey,
who never even lived   in this lawless town named
after him, some story of perishing   in the snow & I know
somehow it's always been   Bodie in our cards—not fields
of Devon violets, but hills   filled with gold
destined to be traded for bones   dressed
in yesterday's best. In Bodie, population zero,   you close
your eyes to revive   the flames that drove miners
& dancers & ministers   from their muslin curtains & firewater,
their harmonicas & pocket   watches, that forced them to set
these scenes   we dismantle with our aimless
coming & going. To be here   is to rehearse
disappearance—or to be here   is to disappear. We enter
a saloon   on whose dusty window's drawn, "Goodbye
God, I'm going to Bodie" & for   one second I feel
the suffering of the dead   is more real
than the suffering   of the living. My friend begins to braid
her long red hair   & a mark looks back at me,
her ear-   lobe pierced some years ago
with gold, its aperture now   traded for a comma-sized shadow.
It feels a little wrong   we've only crossed
one state line to get here & the weather   was prime, the road clear
of snow; likewise wrong that we claim,   as we brush Bodie
from our boots, not to fathom   what possessed so many guests
to hold onto their cursed   stones, nails, globes, jewelflowers,
shards of glass, mattress   springs, a piano once . . .   for years
on end, as if the punishment   were what they were
after   & not the memory of the world

without them in it. I hold   my breath as I walk
Bodie's streets—unaware   of a frail wire in my childhood
home even now being taken   into the mouth
of some small animal; un-   aware the only parts
to survive the heat will be the hearth   & the bathtub, that place
where my body was first   held too close, this head & heart
held underwater like sinners   or sieves, left to warp
but stay   recognizable in that other
ghost town I know   no one pays
to enter or explore—until it burns   so badly I remember
the emptiness I hold   will never belong to me.

IV.

It can only be the end of the world,
as you move forward.
—ARTHUR RIMBAUD

Beginning Wax to Bronze at Chemeketa Community College

I begin applying the Vaseline,
prepping my pig heart for the months-
long transition from flesh
to air to wax to air to bronze.
I want the closest thing to human
I can find & this is it
& I can honestly say I got it for free
from Mt. Angel Meat Company.
Before immersing the muscle
in what dentists use
to capture impressions, I put
my fingers inside & widen
the chambers, make sure
they're big enough to hold a hand-
ful of pencils or fresh cut
orchids. Our teacher, Calvin, tells me
I could make good
money selling these at Saturday
Market, but I've no desire
to share my early attempts.
"Sometimes I think I'm pro-eugenics,"
my friend Susan whispers, her eyes
fixed on our pregnant classmate
who's seated in the corner, naked
from the waist up, slathering her breasts

& belly in plaster of paris. "I mean,
who gets their boobs inked
with barbed wire & flaming dice?"
"Maybe she's religious," the guy next to us
suggests as he eases his pin tool
along the surface of a tiny victory
brown wax gladiator whose chest
plate, he assures us, is completely
accurate. "Don't misunderstand
me," Susan goes on, "I know
my parents should've been sterilized
from the get-go." She's sculpting
a hollow prairie dog that, once
done, will double as an urn & wait
8 months for her father's ticker
to quit. Calvin's decorated
our classroom with classical art
he's torn from a fourteen-month calendar
that began in 1987, the year of
the rabbit & my birth, meaning Venus
de Milo's mutilated perfection flickers
on a yellow sheet under the thrum
of a ventilation fan lately installed
to keep our lungs free
from glass & early
decline. We sometimes enter
a trance, every eye fixed on
a shape it's anxious to see
made void. "I want my corpse

to be a puppet," Susan once
told me. "That way you can be the voice
reading my funeral message, going
something like, 'take a look at my
life, I'm a lot like you.'" I nodded, said
I'd love to be her
voice & have always hoped
for the chance to be a master
of some kind. Calvin's brought us a book
on bronze through the ages & it's making
the rounds. The boy who's forming
a bong, even though he knows
it's not allowed & pretty
toxic to inhale anything
from heated bronze says, "Skip me,"
meaning I get extra time
to linger over a twelfth-century she-wolf.
"Entrapment or decay?" I inquire,
pointing to her gaping
leg, a kind of absence
she seems shaped around, because
I want to know if the artist fucked up
or if this is what happens,
in time, to everything we cast
& the teacher supposes
the maker didn't vent the joint
right, as in, perfectly, & this
should be a lesson to us all. On his neck
what Hippocrates once called

a witch's teat oozes & I consider
how something so minor can kill
a person if ignored. "Get yourself
looked at," I want to say,
but don't. More evidence I'm not
the person I should be. Calvin's
asked me to model
for him. He's being commissioned
by some rich guy in Oahu
to sculpt a female nude surrounded
by blown glass flames rising up
around her & illuminated
blue from below her marble
pedestal. I could be her.
She could have my face, small
breasts & scoliotic spine, or some
version thereof. But I keep this in-
formation to myself—
confidential. I'm getting dirty
looks from my pregnant class-
mate, who's sniffing the air
in dramatic fashion, hoping
I'll reassure everyone
that my reeking under-
taking will subside soon
enough, but in truth
it's barely begun. The book
states the she-wolf was cast
centuries before the murderous

babies were placed
below her swollen teats. Trials
& executions "at the wolf" were
recorded up until 1438, meaning
the she-wolf has seen
more death than you & I
will ever, meaning healing
might always take place
behind closed doors, while
its counterpart requires a public
square be filled with symphonies
of human gasps. Susan
smiles at me. Like most people
I know, she lacks health
& dental. Her left eye
tooth is gray, evidence of a failing
nerve. When she gets
down about her dimming grin,
I remind her my wisdoms
have sunk so low
in my face that I'll start losing
sensation in the near
future. This seems
to help her see me as her
people. "I bought you guys
protection," Calvin announces,
tossing a handful of paper
surgical masks onto the table.
Susan sighs, leans

over & says, "What a joke. We'll all get
cancer in five years
with those face diapers." The mold
around my heart is setting so
slowly, I'll have to leave it
overnight. I pick up one of the masks,
flimsy as an intimate, & try
it on, find myself back at Good
Samaritan's emergency
room, knowing my mother's lungs
are filling with the contents
of her ruptured heart. No.
Aorta. It starts
with a tear in the tunica
intima, that thin robe dressing
a vein from within. She doesn't know
I'm here. She'll never know again.
The doctors ask permission
to revive her with something
chemical & new. I say, yes. I say,
yes. I take the mask off, knowing
how right Susan is. "We're all going
to suffocate down here," I say
& Susan smiles & I glimpse her dying
tooth & she asks, "Did you know Vikings
strangled the slave girls of important
dead men?" as she digs a loop tool
into her wax. The animal's
joints are thick & lack adequate

vents, meaning entrapment
will occur, meaning some part of her
creation won't materialize
under the crucible's tilted lip. "They'd get
all plastered," she continues, "& fuck
the girls & shout out to their gone
master, some version of 'this
is for you!'" "No," I say,
"no, history's never been
my strong suit." When the pregnant
student realizes she's forgotten
the Vaseline, she screams because she can't
pull the shell away
without the sensation of tearing
a giant Band-Aid off. The whole
class, ordering her to breathe,
assumes she's gone into early
labor & who knew all those nearly
invisible hairs covering our hides had
such strength. I wonder when
it began, the belief
that the part of us that's always been
dead keeps growing after what we call
life has left the room.

Underststudy

A maker was once cast   infantine in my arms. It happens
         fast—the body's failed
    cooperation with itself, some little actor ceasing
  to play her part, her past
a sequence of un-applauded performances. As a child, I believed
         perihelion meant *permanently healed,*
as if to near the sun were not to be perforated

by light, but to be relieved of all light's absence
         could reveal. Ironic—how the night
now phases out my face, expressing
   yesterday as tomorrow &, therefore, never
to arrive. I whore myself to another
      patient hour, fashion an arrow from ancestral
    clavicle, a bow from willow & ovine
gut. There's nothing can be called
   irenic in the hunt to come, nor in

the wait, nor in the braiding of one's bloodied hair.
    My sin, like my build, belongs
to some *other*—a mother's father, a feather-
   weight boxer, I'm told,
       whose toxin of choice was parasympathomimetic & left
his visceral pleura dusted gray. He told me once he shot a man
    & if he'd meant to   he would have killed

the bastard. I took his word

as iridic—as in *resistant-to-corrosion*, as in *rare*, as in *elemental-in-
the-face-of-the-earth*. His/my   brow, as he spoke, furrowed

as a field stolen back from switchgrass. I'm told

my smile, too, is on borrow   from his line—Scottish-Irish-
Cherokee. I'm told I've nothing of my father

drifting in my veins, no Maya nor marimba nor

conquistadores. I get the sense I'm altering

the forecast. I get the sense   what's caroming round

my skull is a system I don't want to name.

Private Lessons

The third thing I learned
       was to surround myself with ample
space. My teacher bound

my toes in turquoise tape—type an ovine
       foot requires when trouble nests
within. I'd bow at close of class, as if I weren't

       the only one allowed
inside the room. He went by Cloud
       & had designs on dying

soon. Each week, another noun
       gone missing from his mouth. I
mean, a tooth defined

       by a "toxic" crown.
I think I thought that he divined the ground
       when he said, "Don't

look at the floor: it's just a sign
       you don't trust me
to tell you if it disappears." He wound around

his throat each day camphoric
        scarves & I resigned what all I could
to expert touch & expiration. He would crouch

at my blistered feet, a sweat-
        stained supplicant bent
on aligning my frame with his fever

        dream, bent on forming a farmer's
daughter into a true
        danseuse. What use

in maligning his methods now? His name
        is just a sound
I hear in sleep. "Hate

the sin, but not
        the sinner," said a God-
fearer at his service, as to astound, as to revive

rumors of unkempt relations. Our inner-
        most contours grew a little
too perceptible & pleasing

to our eyes. Sure, we'd found
        a reciprocity: he knew
the breadwinner in my family couldn't win

much, so he'd taken me
          on for a song—no faltering
in it. He'd set me spinning

          round him while he clapped. Call it keeping
time. Call it manáge. Reader,
          we worked with our wrong

deadline, too full
          of ourselves & an ability to make
an artful thing. I was twelve. He held

          my spine at start
of class & gave a practiced
          jerk, mock broke my neck in the name

of a pleasing line. Him, swallowed up
          in crimson robe. Me, supine in nude leotard. "Stop
moving," he said, but his palsies unwound

in my heel & bowed arch. He's managed to stay
          as ache. In the wood box, cinder.
The first thing I learned was to hold my tongue.

Next to Nothing

         I subtract myself
from the shadow of an ash tree, knowing well
        my life is not yet right-
fully mine, nor is it   what I'd deem old, though it has
          moved the meat of me
  beyond the beginning. I press   my ear to
my father's field, the one he's turned, the one he'll be
      ceding to the unappeasable—no matter.

       Some stories only toll
in the mind. I tell myself   no one will erase herself
from the life of a child I don't   yet have and never will. Still,
     terror keeps her cursive   records in the end
         table, her bottles full of untouched
tablets under the sink; and I keep a frayed
       armchair that holds   the shape of
  nobody on earth. I have tried to preserve the sense of
     beginning. Once, I troubled to catch a still
image in which a pair of hands (I have them   memorized) frenzied
          over their instrument (inherited
upright, keys so old they were souvenirs of re-
         creational slaughter). It seemed
each finger held its own
      appetite, tendons tensed toward any given
   song's requirements (accidental, half-
rest, augmented   fifth, diminished   seventh, now

another rest, then   repeat, then   repeat) that, if not
        met, would whisper flaw   into any ready ear,
but there were so few at hand, often
                only my own, on occasion a sheep
with a bell fastened to her   muddy throat who, having broken
    from the pasture, led   her bleating population to the open
        window when my mother played. Like a joke,
she said,   like some cartoon
            scene in which nature assembles
at the singing   maiden's bare feet. Half the images proved over-
        or double-   exposed, the other
half full of   hands, uncaptured—all
        hyaline, moving at the speed of sight, its artificial
instrument that *is*, and the ring   fevered into bolts
        of Z's, the light   writing its brevity
            over the keys, the keys rising up
through a chorus of fingers   hymning, mad (blue
            capillary Y   almost illegible). It was a manual
device—a little faulty and in need   of a steady hand. Mine
                held nothing close to still.

If She Stands Still, She Is Dancing

Everything is here
        in this furrowed vale,
a girl the world might call
        a blemish lying
in dust, her slip lit up
        with late day sun. She make-believes
she's never been here
        before, that luck has left her
in this field. She knows the stream
        is close and running low, its surface
animating crane flies, their numb
        forms fluttering for miles.
The light finds a way
        through her lids, stains the hour
orange, and the scent
        of dry pines stays so present
it starts to disappear. All the beauty
        she will ever need
has visited itself upon her.
        Drag her by her braided hair
into a room that smells of soap.
        Heaven will go with her. Hold her
until stillness is a vow.
        Whatever she does next is a dance.

Gallowed Be

The nearest land-   fill's nowhere
        near & no one is
to blame. We burn the year's
news—in the meadow, in the mind,
    till the crosswords & the funnies wilt
to winterkill. I trace
        the day an epitaph
in ash: "Hallowed Be
        Thy Games." Every story is
ashamed to be true. My father's now
    a widower & no one
is to blame. My sister
        doesn't laugh, plots to live
on land turned tame—where the soil's kissed
with concrete, yields no wine.
    It's all the same   to me, if we winnow,
        if we win. I tell
    myself the story that I'll visit
distant cisterns, let their sallow
        walls win me over, lift my low
life & lowly frame   of mind. My father
        gets fined for burning out
of season, says he doesn't
get why. So   the days go slow & I
        climb a pulsing fence that stops
no bucks nor does, observe

the neighbor's piglets wallow
in their loam. (Still,
the world is   wide, if the hymnal's hold
true,   & every beast has a mind   to get loose
from a valley fallowing
toward foul.) My sister   braids my waist-
length mane, says, "This
place is   lame." I try to tell her
no one is to blame, but the sky is
so hollow it swallows every name.

Notes

"Philomath" means "lover of learning" or "love of learning" in Greek. I have privileged the latter definition in this collection, given the fact that the town of Philomath, Oregon, uses that definition in its public signage.

"Curse of Bodie" refers to W. S. Bodey never having lived in the town of Bodie, not because he didn't live in the geographical spot that became the town of Bodie, but because it was not a town, and as such was unnamed, during his lifetime.

Acknowledgments

Bennington Review: "Golden" and "Curse of Bodie"

Best New Poets 2019: "Private Lessons"

BOAAT: "Out of Body" (I envy the air...)

Copper Nickel: "Out of Body" (have you ever watched a person burn...)

The Harvard Advocate: "Ascent"

jubilat: "My Materia"

Narrative: "We Said Our Common Ancestor Was Eve"

New England Review: "Philomath"
and "Beginning Wax to Bronze at Chemeketa Community College"

Ploughshares: "Damp Room"

Poetry: "After Birth"

Poetry Northwest: "Kings Valley," "The Blood's Unwritable Psalm,"
and "Out of Body" (How many times...)

The Poetry Review: "Gallowed Be"

Poet's Country: "Permission to Mar"

The Rumpus: "Of Gut & Gold"

The Scores: "Gray Diggers"

West Branch Wired: "Persistence of Vision"

To Sally Keith for seeing worth in these pages and for selecting *Philomath* for publication with Milkweed through the National Poetry Series. This is the greatest honor of my life.

To Daniel Slager and to Joanna Demkiewicz, Bailey Hutchinson, Claire Laine, Milan Wilson-Robinson, and everyone at Milkweed who works so tirelessly and with such integrity and vision on behalf of literature. Thank you for welcoming me to Milkweed and for bringing *Philomath* to life.

To Mary Austin Speaker for giving *Philomath* the most beautiful form I could have possibly imagined for it.

To my teachers and mentors, heroes all. To Jeremy Trabue, Steve Slemenda, Karelia Stetz-Waters, and Tammy Jabin of Chemeketa Community College for nurturing my obsession with literature. To Michael Koch, my advisor at Cornell and the first person to encourage me to pursue a life in writing. Your words have seen me through some difficult times. To Mark Wunderlich and Michael Dumanis of Bennington College for expanding my sense of what the poetic line could do and be, for understanding the necessity of poetry to our lives, and for giving me the tools and the permission necessary to begin writing this book. To Mark Levine, James Gavin, and Elizabeth Willis of the Iowa Writers' Workshop; your deep readings of poems and meticulous line edits inspired me as both a writer and editor. Thank you for your wisdom and for living the poetry you teach. To Jane Mead for helping order this collection and for being such a genuine and honest mentor and friend. To Shane McCrae, Stephanie Burt, Robyn Schiff, and Nick Twemlow for your enduring encouragement, generosity, and all-around brilliance. I look up to you something crazy.

To all the editors who first believed in these poems. And a very special thanks to Rick Barot for changing my life by selecting "Philomath" for publication in the *New England Review*.

To Jennifer Grotz and everyone at Bread Loaf. You have reinvented Mount Olympus in Vermont, and I want to live there all the time.

To Keith Leonard and Noah Warren for reading and offering invaluable feedback on early drafts of *Philomath*. I'm forever in your debt.

To the Bucknell Seminar for Undergraduate Poets and the Community of Writers for providing time, space, and structure that I badly needed in order to finish the first draft of this book.

To Jill Davis and to NYU's Creative Writing Program for supporting my continued writing endeavors through the Jill Davis Fellowship. And to Deborah Landau, Joyce Carol Oates, and John Freeman for being such generous mentors and supporters of this book during my time at NYU.

To my family. To my mother, Jackie. Your generosity, dedication, and passion came through in everything you did, from gathering the folktales of steam-age loggers to teaching your daughters how to read music. You are loved and missed every single day. To my father, Frank, dreamer, natural-born storyteller, and the first person in this world to make me laugh; and to my sister, Tara, my best and oldest friend: without you two, this book would not exist. To Joan Boening for welcoming me into her family and giving me a space to live and write after leaving Iowa. (Many a poem in this book was edited in your living room!)

And to my husband, Justin. Thank you for being the brilliant and no-bullshit first reader that you are—and for encouraging me to keep writing these home town poems. You deserve to have a thousand acres of trees planted in your honor. And a bridge (preferably over a large and turbulent river) named after you.

Kenneth Barton

DEVON WALKER-FIGUEROA is originally from Kings Valley, a ghost town in the Oregon Coast Range. She is a graduate of the Iowa Writers' Workshop and the 2018 recipient of the *New England Review*'s Emerging Writer Award. Her poems have appeared in such publications as *The Nation, Poetry*, the *American Poetry Review, Lana Turner,* and *Ploughshares.*

milkweed
editions

Founded as a nonprofit organization in 1980, Milkweed Editions is an independent publisher. Our mission is to identify, nurture and publish transformative literature, and build an engaged community around it.

Milkweed Editions is based in Bdé Óta Othúŋwe (Minneapolis) within Mní Sota Makhóčhe, the traditional homeland of the Dakhóta people. Residing here since time immemorial, Dakhóta people still call Mní Sota Makhóčhe home, with four federally recognized Dakhóta nations and many more Dakhóta people residing in what is now the state of Minnesota. Due to continued legacies of colonization, genocide, and forced removal, generations of Dakhóta people remain disenfranchised from their traditional homeland. Presently, Mní Sota Makhóčhe has become a refuge and home for many Indigenous nations and peoples, including seven federally recognized Ojibwe nations. We humbly encourage our readers to reflect upon the historical legacies held in the lands they occupy.

milkweed.org

Interior Design by Tijqua Daiker and Mary Austin Speaker

Typeset in Adobe Jenson

Adobe Jenson was designed by Robert Slimbach for Adobe
and released in 1996. Slimbach based Jenson's roman styles
on a text face cut by fifteenth-century type designer Nicolas Jenson,
and its italics are based on type created by Ludovico Vicentino
degli Arrighi, a late fifteenth-century papal scribe
and type designer.